D0317657

Published 2012 by
Bloomsbury Publishing Plc
50 Bedford Square, London, WC1B 3DP

www.bloomsbury.com
www.storiesfromthezoo.com

ISBN 978-1-4081-6051-0

Picture acknowledgements:
Cover images: Shutterstock
Inside images all Shutterstock apart from the following:
p5 inset ©ZSL, p8 inset ©ZSL/Gambia Bolton, p8-9 main ©ZSL, p9 top right inset
©ZSL, p9 bottom right inset ©Chip, skuterhijau.blogspot.com, p11 inset ©ZSL,
p19 bottom right inset by Ernst Stavro Blofeld via Wikimedia Commons, p46 inset
©Cheetah Conservation Fund, www.cheetah.org, p55 top inset ©Northern Jaguar
Project/Naturalia, www.northernjaguarproject.org, p56-57 ©James Godwin/Cat
Survival Trust, p77 middle inset ©James Godwin/Cat Survival Trust.

Manufactured and supplied under licence from the Zoological Society of London.

Produced for Bloomsbury Publishing Plc by Gridlock Design
www.gridlock-design.co.uk

A CIP catalogue for this book is available from the British Library.

Printed in China by C&C Offset Printing Co.

MIX
Paper from
responsible sources
FSC® C008047

Michael Cox

BIG CATS

Terrifyingly terrific big cat facts

CONTENTS

INTRODUCTION

SUPER CATS!

IMAGINE BEING ABLE TO...

- Knock down a galloping zebra with one blow of your hand!
- Roar so loud you can be heard eight kilometres (five miles) away
- Run at 110 kilometres (70 miles) an hour
- See in the dark
- Disappear in the blink of an eye
- Hear the smallest sound from 100 metres (330 feet) away
- Waggle your ears
- Carry objects three times your own weight
- Jump as high as a two-storey house
- Bite right through a cow's skull
- Leap six metres (20 feet) across a ravine

Between them, big cats can do all of these things and more! These awesome feline **predators** really are super cats!

A domestic cat marking its territory

BIG CATS IN THE WILD

The lives of big cats in the wild are very similar in many ways. Apart from lions, which live in groups called **prides**, all other wild cats live on their own, hunt alone and only briefly get together to mate. As soon as the cubs are grown, mother and children will all go their separate ways, to live out their own big cat lives.

Another thing that all wild big cats do, and small pet ones for that matter, is to mark out their **territories** by weeing and pooing on what they consider to be the edges of their **'domains'** in order to warn other cats to keep out. They will also scratch at trees and rocks and mark them with their body scent for the same reason.

KEEP OUT

BIG CATS IN CAPTIVITY

Many people used to think that keeping wild animals in zoos was cruel. But opinions have changed. Firstly, because the conditions in which animals are kept are so much better than they used to be. And secondly, because breeding from captive animals is a crucial way of preserving **many species that are in danger of becoming** extinct in the wild.

The bad old days of zoos

A HOME FROM HOME

In the 'bad old days', big cats were kept in small, bare cages, where there wasn't room to swing a cat! But nowadays zoos understand a lot more about the needs of cats and go out of their way to create stimulating and comfortable living conditions which are just like places in the wild. For example, in order to design the new Sumatran tiger enclosure at ZSL London Zoo, zoologists from the Zoo will be visiting the Sumatran jungle so that they can study it in detail and recreate a 'piece of it' back in England.

KEEPING FIT

In the wild, big cats leap, climb and run as they hunt their **prey**, so to make up for the fact that this doesn't happen in captivity, zoos provide big cats with all sorts of exercise toys and 'keep-fit' routines. These include things like meat-filled balls on bungee ropes and amazing devices which get cheetahs running and tigers leaping. Food, such as chickens and rabbits, is also given to big cats whole with the feathers or fur still on, or is buried or frozen in blocks of ice, so that they really have to work in order to get their meals.

Go on, dare you, take it off me!

A Sumatran tiger getting some exercise

BIG CATS AND THEIR KEEPERS

Big cat carers know that big cats, just like people, have their own personalities. All keepers quickly form a relationship with the cats they care for, and because they understand their moods, they can develop ways of keeping them calm and happy.

For instance, if a tiger is a little bit anxious, the keeper will blink at it slowly, because tigers don't like to be fixed with an unbroken stare. This reassures the tiger and it soon begins to blink back at its keeper, its **body language** showing that it has calmed down.

HEALTH CHECKS

Big cats at zoos are checked daily for signs of illness and are regularly **vaccinated** to prevent them catching diseases. If they are found to be suffering in any way, an expert is called in and everything is done to make them well again, be it an operation by a vet, or a visit from the big cat dentist.

Care starts almost immediately with big cats born in captivity. When they're about four weeks old, big cat cubs are vaccinated and implanted with an identity **micro-chip**. To do this, the fiercely protective mum is distracted with food. Before her cubs are returned to her they are rubbed down with bedding straw so she doesn't detect the smell of the keeper on them and reject them.

Big cats live much longer in captivity than they do in the wild. If a big cat in captivity is really suffering, they're gently 'put to sleep' by a vet. Whichever way they go, it always leaves the big cat keepers feeling heartbroken.

Even panthers need dentists!

Surgery at ZSL London Zoo

1 TIGERS

THE WORLD'S FAVOURITE ANIMAL

Tigers are big cat superstars! In a poll of 50,000 people held in 73 different countries, the tiger was voted the world's favourite animal. With their fabulous stripes, glowing eyes, graceful movements and supremely powerful bodies, they are truly magnificent!

Tigers live in Eastern and Southeast Asia where they prowl forests, **mangrove swamps** and open grasslands. The largest sort of tiger is the Siberian, or Amur as it's also called. Sadly, there are only about 450 of these in the wild. The largest Siberian tiger ever seen was a humongous four metres (13 feet) long!

The Bengal or Indian tiger is the most common sort, but there are still only about 1,850 Bengal tigers in the wild. The Sumatran tiger is the smallest type of tiger but they're still around two and a half metres (seven to eight feet) long.

BITE-SIZE MORSEL

When they're looking at tiger and lion skeletons side-by-side even big cat experts struggle to tell them apart. It's only the fur that really helps them to tell which is which.

MAKING A SPLASH

Tigers are powerful swimmers and have been known to swim distances of more than 20 kilometres (12 miles). In Southeast Asia, tigers spend much of their time in rivers or swamps, feeding on fish or turtles. Although they like water, tigers don't like getting it in their eyes, and because of this will often walk backwards into a river.

Tigers are super swimmers

THE CUTAWAY TIGER

Collar bone or clavicle: Extra small so that it 'floats' between the shoulder blades. This allows the tiger to take really long strides.

Eyes: Large lenses and pupils. Reflective **retina** which aids night vision.

Back teeth or carnassials: Used to cut meat like knife blades. Tigers swallow large pieces of meat whole (tut, tut, no manners!)

Tongue: Covered in sharp 'sticky-out-bits' for grooming and stripping meat from bones.

Facial whiskers: About fifteen centimetres (six inches) long. The Sumatran tiger has the most face whiskers.

Canine teeth: From six and a half to seven and a half centimetres (two and a half to three inches) in length. Tigers have the largest canines of all big cat species.

Small front teeth or incisors: Used to pluck feathers and to clean meat off the bone.

The dewclaw: This claw never touches the ground and is used as a 'thumb' for grasping prey.

Body size: Up to four metres (13 feet) long and can weigh as much as 295 kilograms (650 pounds).

Height: Shoulder height of up to one metre (three and a half feet).

Backbone: Very flexible, so that the tiger can twist and turn during chases.

Stripes: Most tigers have over 100 ranging from black to grey or brown.

Fur: Rusty-red to yellow ochre in colour. Lighter underparts.

Tail: Up to one point two metres (four feet) long, and ringed with dark bands. Used for balance and communication.

Stomach: Short intestines and a small, light stomach because meat needs less digestion than plants.

Feet: Huge and padded for silent stalking. Tigers walk on their toes.

Claws: Five on each foot, all **retractable** so that they stay razor sharp.

WATCH OUT, THERE'S A TIGER ABOUT

It's night in the jungle and it's very, very dark. Animals are looking for food, or trying to find a safe place to spend the night. All at once, they go quiet. A tiger is on the prowl!

All the animals are at risk of being eaten by this massive predator. From the smallest mice to the biggest buffalo. The animals listen for the slightest noise, which may warn of a tiger's approach. But the tiger's padded paws make sure its movements are silent.

Many of the animals are really well camouflaged, and in the darkness they are almost invisible. But the tiger's eyes, with their extra large lenses and pupils can spot the slightest movement.

The tiger's amazingly sensitive ears pick up a rustling sound, and its super-sensitive whiskers detect a tiny disturbance in the air pressure. Some wild pigs are on the move!

A terrified piglet breaks from the group and races into the forest. The tiger explodes into action, covering an astonishing ten metres (30 feet) per second!

The piglet is running for its life, desperate to escape the mighty killing machine just metres behind it. As the tiger runs, its tail swishes wildly from side to side, helping it keep its balance as it performs lightning fast twists and turns.

The tiger now leaps an incredible ten metres, (30 feet) falling upon its prey, and sinking its huge canines into its spine.

The struggle is over. The tiger uses its teeth to slice and devour huge chunks of meat. A successful hunt!

And this little piggy is... dinner!

A tiger on the prowl

SAVING THE TIGER

During the 19th century, people were killing tigers in India like there was no tomorrow. In one place alone, an English army colonel shot 158 tigers in just four years! Even though those bad old days of tiger slaughter are gone, there are still problems. In the 1960s there were 40 million people in India. Now there are 1.2 billion. And they all need something to eat and somewhere to live. So what do they do? They move into a bit more tiger habitat.

Not only are tigers losing their habitat to farmers, loggers and towns, they are also still hunted for their body parts which are used in Asian medicines. For example, tiger flesh is said to give courage and strength to those who eat it, a tiger's collar bone is used to ward off evil, and tiger brain is mixed with oil and rubbed on to the body to cure spots and, would you believe it... laziness!

There are now less than 3,200 tigers living in the wild in the whole world. However, things are now being done to help tigers. For instance, in the 1970s, India began passing laws against killing tigers. And in Indonesia, ZSL has launched a tiger anti-poaching unit in Berbak National Park. As well as educating the local people about the importance of protecting tigers, wardens patrol the tiger habitat areas to stop poachers killing any more tigers. In China, **conservationists** are now reintroducing young tigers born in captivity back into the wild after they've been taught hunting skills in a process known as rewilding.

HOMELESS
PLEASE HELP

Sorry, no room for tigers here!

A 19th century hunter and his kill

TWELVE TERRIFIC TIGER FACTS

1 Tigers, just like domestic pet cats, eat grass to help with their digestion and to bring up fur balls.

2 Tigers shed their hair once or twice a year. Their coat is short in the summer and long in the winter.

3 Scientists examining the contents of tigers' stomachs have found bear claws and porcupine quills in them.

4 Tiger spit is antiseptic. They lick their wounds to stop infections entering them.

5 Tigers are very fussy about keeping clean. They use their big tongues to remove loose hairs and dirt from their coat. They also lick their paws and then wash their heads, just like pet cats do.

王

6 The stripes on the top of a tiger's head make a pattern just like the Chinese 'wang' symbol, which means 'king'.

7 If a tiger is feeling chilled out, its tail droops. When it meets a pal, it raises its tail and waves it slowly. If it's miffed, it holds it low, occasionally twitching it or frantically swishing it from side to side.

8 Tigers have long whiskers dotted around different parts of their body which sense nearby objects and changes in air pressure, just as their facial whiskers do.

9 In the days when tigers were hunted mercilessly, their super-sensitive hearing enabled them to pick up the sound of a gun being loaded. They learned to associate this sound with trouble and escape.

10 Like whales, tigers can communicate using low **infrasound** which cannot be detected by the human ear. This is really useful for communicating with other tigers which are a long way away, as infrasound passes straight through dense forests, rocks, and even mountains!

11 The striped pattern on tigers' fur goes right through to their skin, so if you shaved a tiger, it would still be striped.

12 Just as all humans have fingerprints which are special to them only, each and every single tiger in the world has its own unique pattern of camouflage stripes.

TIGERS: FAST FACTS

Where they live: small areas in Asia

Habitat: tropical rainforests, snow covered forests, mangrove swamps

Length: largest – Siberian tiger, average male 3 metres (10 feet) long, smallest – Sumatran tiger, average male 2.4 metres (8 feet) long

Weight: Siberian tiger, average male 181 kilograms (400 pounds)

Life span: 15 to 20 years in the wild, up to 26 years in zoos

Number of young at birth: average 2 to 3

Size at birth: 1 kilogram (2.2 pounds)

Status: all wild tigers are endangered

Asia

A tiger in the garden!

SAFETY TIPS

If a Siberian tiger unexpectedly turns up in your back garden (don't laugh, these things can happen you know), whatever you do, don't turn your back on it and run away. Doing that would just activate its natural urge to chase you and you would be pounced on in a flash. What you must do is face the tiger and make lots of noise, then slowly back away from it. Piece of cake!

SOMETHING TO GET YOUR CLAWS INTO

Tigers have huge curved claws which enable them to hold onto large prey. They also use them to climb up trees head-first. The only problem is that because tigers are such big and heavy creatures, they find it really difficult to get back down again. So they either have to jump out of the tree or crawl down backwards (which makes them look really daft). This may explain why tigers hardly ever climb trees.

2 LIONS

THE ROAR TRUTH

There are lions in London's Trafalgar Square. But they're just carved ones. However, in the early 1990s, a real lion's toe bone was dug up quite near to Trafalgar Square's famous lion statues during building work. It belonged to one of the hundreds of lions which used to roam the banks of the River Thames along with rhinos and hippos some 10,000 years ago.

In fact, back then, there were so many lions in the world that the only mammals which exceeded them in number were human beings. But, due to things like being wiped out by various ice ages and hunted to extinction, lions now only live in the wild in Africa, south of the Sahara desert, and in one small forest in India.

In the caves at Lascaux in France there are pictures of local lions which were painted 15,000 years ago by Paleolithic people.

The Sri Lankan flag

Lions are associated with strength, courage, nobility and gentleness and their images appear all over the place, on coats of arms, on flags (like the Sri Lankan flag), on all the doors of the Forbidden City in Beijing, and even on tins of golden syrup, computer operating systems, rugby shirts and chickens' eggs!

Lions in London! These famous lions in Trafalgar Square won't hurt you

ONE BIG HAPPY FAMILY... WELL, ALMOST!

Lions are more sociable than any other sort of big cat, (and regularly challenge other lions to games of cricket or go on family outings to the seaside). While all other wild cats mainly live on their own, lions live in family groups known as prides (and are very proud to do so).

Prides can consist of anything from just one male and one female to a couple of males, (which are known as a **coalition**), and five or six related females, along with a dozen or so cubs. The lionesses cleverly time their breeding so that they all give birth to their cubs at around the same time. This means they can share parenting duties such as feeding, washing and teaching their cubs to hunt. The female cubs become part of the pride, but when the male cubs reach maturity they have to go off into the wild and fend for themselves.

A pride of lions in the African savanah

A coalition! The boys are back in town

The family unit doesn't remain one big happy family for long though, because the male lions at the head of the pride are often challenged by younger males from outside, who are intent on taking over their females. If an outsider manages to beat the ruling male in a fight, then he will take over the pride and kill all the existing cubs so he can start new families of his own. So most male lions only manage to remain in charge of a pride for two years at most. Cripes, it's a jungle out there!

WOOF?

Lions make about 12 different sorts of sounds including woofs, grunts, snarls, hisses, moans, puffs and, most famously... ROARS!

A male lion's roar is so loud that it can be heard up to eight kilometres (five miles) away by human ears and further than that by other lions. Lions roar for several reasons, including warning off enemies, protecting territory, calling to other pride members (and getting audiences to sit up and pay attention at the movies).

Mum lions grunt to call their cubs. When a lion 'puffs' it makes a sound like a held-in sneeze and does it to let other lions know that it's friendly. Lions also show affection to other lions by rubbing up against them and licking their ears, face and shoulders. However, when a lion is angry it will press its ears flat against its head and snarl or roar menacingly.

THE 'MANE' ATTRACTION

Most adult male lions sport the enormous freaky hair-do known as their mane. One of its jobs is to attract mates, and lionesses are particularly attracted by lions who have really thick, dark manes.

Manes also make male lions look larger than they actually are when they're taking on big beasts such as rhinos, buffalo and other lions.

When male lions do get to scrapping, they're more likely to bite a mouthful of mane than a chunk of flesh. Manes do have disadvantages though. They stand out a bit too much when male lions are creeping up on prey and can get very uncomfortable on extra hot days. (They're also a complete nightmare to shampoo and style!)

THE LIONS' SHARE

Lions mainly eat the hoofed animals which are known as ungulates and include creatures such as wildebeest, buffalo, springbok, zebra and Thomson's gazelles. They also eat hippos, giraffes, warthogs, birds, pythons, other lions, young elephants, crocodiles, baboons, chimpanzees and fish. Lions living on the coast of the African country of Namibia also eat fur seals and cormorants.

Lions are the only big cats that hunt as a team, and it's the lionesses, which are smaller, faster and more **agile**, who usually do the hunting.

The pride starts out by loosely fanning out as they search for prey. As they do, they all act quite casually, as if to say, 'What us? Looking to tear you limb from limb and devour you in huge bloody chunks. Oh come off it, mate! We're just enjoying an early morning stroll.'

However, the moment a lioness spots a potential victim, she freezes or sinks down and all the other lionesses do exactly the same. Then they begin to **stalk** the prey, crawling towards it with their bellies touching the ground.

A lioness with her kill

When they are in striking distance, they silently burst from cover and race towards their prey. One of the hugely powerful lionesses will jump on its back, then crush the victim's windpipe while the other lionesses hold it down. Sometimes, quite gruesomely, the other lions begin eating the victim before it's dead.

The scene around a lion kill is quite revolting. If the pride males are around they get to eat first followed by the lionesses, then the cubs (not very 'new lion', are they?)

HUNTERS TURNED GAMEKEEPERS

In the last 20 years or so between 30 per cent and 50 per cent of African lions have disappeared. The destruction of their habitat and being killed by humans are definitely two reasons for their decline. As a result, some lions are now what is described as a 'vulnerable' species (although if you were locked in a room with half a dozen you'd probably find this hard to believe).

One reason lions are killed by humans is because they attack herds of livestock. Some of the Maasai warriors of Kenya and Tanzania who have hunted lions for hundreds of years in order to protect their cattle, sheep and goats now take part in the 'Lion Guardians' conservation project. They use their brilliant tracking skills to watch and monitor lions for their well-being, as well as peacefully sorting out problems involving lions killing domestic animals.

Maasai warriors of Kenya

LIONS: FAST FACTS

Where they live: parts of Africa and the Gir Forest in India

Habitat: grassy plains, open woodland, savannas, scrubland

Body length: males 1.7 to 2.5 metres (5.6 to 8.3 feet), females 1.4 to 1.7 metres (4.6 to 5.7 feet)

Tail length: 70 to 105 centimetres (27 to 41 inches)

Shoulder height: males 1.2 metres (4 feet), females one metre (3.5 feet)

Weight: males 150 to 250 kilograms (330 to 550 pounds), females 120 to 180 kilograms (265 to 400 pounds)

Life span: 15 years in the wild, up to 30 in zoos

Number of young at birth: 3 to 4

Size at birth: 1.5 kilograms (3 pounds)

Status: the Asian lion is endangered and the African lion is classed as 'vulnerable'

Africa

TEN TREMENDOUS LION FACTS

1 Lions dig more than other big cats and unearth and kill warthogs, which live in abandoned anteater burrows.

4 In some African **game reserves**, lions have learned to attack giraffes when they're walking on roads because the giraffes find it harder to stay upright on smooth tarmac.

2 Lions can swim quite well and sometimes cross wide rivers such as the mighty Okavango in Africa.

3 In the 20th century, witch doctors in parts of Africa terrified people by telling them that if they didn't pay them 'protection money' they would turn into lions and attack them. People who didn't pay were killed by men dressed as lions wearing real lion paw gloves on their hands and feet... complete with claws!

5 King Henry I of England (1069–1135) kept a **menagerie** of exotic beasts including lions, which was later moved to the Tower of London.

6 When the famous composer, Amadeus Mozart (1756–1791) was taken to see the lions in the Tower, he was so frightened that he burst into tears. But he was only eight at the time.

Stay calm! We'll have you out in a jiffy

7 After losing his job as a priest, the Rector of Stiffkey ended up working at a fun fair in Skegness where he did a 'Daniel in the Lions' Den' act with a lion called Freddie and a lioness called Toto. After accidentally tripping over Toto's tail during a performance he was attacked by Freddie and died of his injuries a few days later.

8 The Ancient Egyptians managed to exterminate their entire lion population by 1100 BC. Pharaoh Amenhotep III killed more than 100 lions in a single hunt.

9 In 2004 a mummified lion was found in the tomb of King Tutankhamen's nurse.

10 The ancient Roman **naturalist** Pliny said that a lion will not attack anyone who humbly lies down in front of it. After you, Mr Pliny!

3 CHEETAHS

A SUPER-FAST, SPOTTED, SPEED MACHINE

As well as being the fastest land animal in the world, the cheetah is also the least dangerous of the big cats. There is no record of a cheetah ever having killed a human. Nevertheless, they are still persecuted and killed by people. As a result they are now an endangered species.

At one time there were cheetahs all over Africa and large parts of Asia and, even about a hundred years ago, there were still at least 100,000 cheetahs living in the wild. There are now less than 12,000 left! These elegant, high-speed sprinters live mainly in Africa where they inhabit grasslands and plains. Asiatic cheetahs used to range across Arabia and through Iran and India. Now they are only found in a small part of Iran and there are very few left. They are the last of their kind.

Cheetahs mainly hunt in the daytime, unlike most other big cats, which are either nocturnal, or crepuscular, which means they're active at dusk and dawn.

CHEETAHS: FAST FACTS

Where they live: parts of Africa and a very small part of Iran (Asia)

Habitat: grasslands and open plains

Shoulder height: 67 to 94 centimetres (2 to 3 feet)

Length: 1 to 1.4 metres (3.6 to 4.4 feet)

Tail length: 66 to 84 centimetres (26 to 33 inches)

Weight: 39 to 65 kilograms (86 to 143 pounds), with males larger than females

Life span: up to 12 years in the wild, 17 in zoos

Number of young at birth: usually 3 to 5

Size at birth: 150 to 300 grams (5 to 10 ounces)

Status: vulnerable

Iran (Asia)

Africa

A HUNTER'S BEST FRIEND?

Captive cheetahs are quite easy to tame and hunters in ancient civilisations, such as Egypt and Sumeria, went in search of prey with a cheetah sitting behind them on their horse. The cheetah wore a hood and was perched on a cushion.

The moment the prey was sighted the hunter would whip off the cheetah's hood and set it in pursuit of their victim (the cheetah, not the hood). Then, in a positive explosion of energy and power, reaching speeds of 112 kilometres (70 miles) an hour, the cheetah would chase down the animal, finally clamping its jaws on its throat and strangling it to death.

European nobles have also hunted with cheetahs for nearly a thousand years. And, in parts of India, using cheetahs for hunting was still going on right until the middle of the twentieth century.

The Egyptian pharaohs believed the cheetah was a goddess named Mafdet and kept them as companions. They also believed that the cheetah would carry their soul to the afterworld.

The 16th century Indian ruler Akbar the Great kept an astonishing total of 9,000 pet cheetahs during his 49 year reign and made detailed records of their behaviour. However he only succeeded in breeding a single litter of cubs from them.

THE HUNTER BECOMES THE HUNTED

It's not just humans who pose a huge threat to cheetahs in the wild. It's other animals, too. One of the reasons cheetahs hunt in the daytime is to avoid the nocturnal, and more powerful, leopards and lions which would easily kill them and their cubs.

Mother cheetahs in particular have their work cut out protecting their offspring. They usually give birth to between three and five cubs about three months after mating, then keep the cubs hidden from predators in a burrow. And they don't get much help from dad. Once they've mated, male cheetahs often leave the female, either living on their own or in groups of three or four brothers known as coalitions. However, coalitions do occasionally stay around and help out if cubs are attacked.

When they're about five weeks old, the cubs begin to share their mother's food in addition to drinking her milk. Then, when they're about three months old, mum brings small, live prey animals back to the den so they can learn to chase and kill them. But all the while she is constantly watching out for the hyenas, wild dogs, lions, baboons, eagles and other animals that regularly kill and eat cheetah cubs. Sadly, up to 90 per cent of cubs are killed by predators in the early part of their lives. Who'd be a cheetah!

'Cor, it's big out here!

Cheetah verses vulture

THE CUTAWAY CHEETAH

Head: Small with flat face and short muzzle.

Lungs: Huge, essential for keeping large amounts of oxygen flowing to the cheetah's muscles.

Eyes: Large with a wide, super-sensitive stripe on the retina which gives the cheetah pin-sharp wide angle and binocular vision.

Nose: Big flared nostrils with large air-filled **sinuses**.

Body: Narrow and lightweight with long slender legs and feet for speed and agility.

Heart: Large and powerful.

Paw pads: Tough and hard, these are quite similar to tyre treads.

Liver: Oversized for storing and creating large amounts of energy-giving **glucose**.

Body size: Up to about one and a half metres long (four and a half feet) and can weigh up to 65 kilograms (143 pounds).

Height: Shoulder height of up to 94 centimetres (three feet).

Arteries: Large and strong to circulate blood from the cheetah's heart to the rest of its body as quickly as possible.

Spine: Incredibly flexible to allow the cheetah's legs greater reach.

Hips and shoulders: Loose and flexible, allowing cheetahs to perform astonishing twists and turns as they run.

Tail: Long and muscular, this is used for balance, stopping the cheetah skidding off course during high-speed chases.

Colouring: Tan or buff coat with black spots makes for excellent camouflage on the grasslands where the cheetah hunts.

Claws: Short, blunt and semi-retractable, these grip the ground like the studs on an athlete's running shoes.

ON YOUR MARKS, GET SET, GO!

How a cheetah pursues its prey, achieving zero to 70 miles per hour in just seconds; leaving most modern sports cars standing!

1 The cheetah is walking slowly through grassland looking for gazelles, warthogs, hare, or one of its other favourite prey animals.

2 It sees a herd of gazelles and now moves through the grass in a semi-crouch until it's within 70 metres (230 feet) of the herd.

3 The gazelles now spot the cheetah and take off like the wind. The cheetah is up and running!

4 In its first three strides, the cheetah accelerates from zero to an amazing 64 kilometres (40 miles) per hour!

5 Then, in just seconds, it reaches its full speed of 110 kilometres (70 miles) per hour!

6 As it runs, only one foot touches the ground at a time.

7 At two points in the cheetah's seven to eight metre (20 to 25 foot) stride, none of its feet are touching the ground.

8 Now, achieving full speed, the cheetah is taking between 60 and 150 breaths per minute! Its entire body is working to its absolute limit.

9 It catches up with a fleeing gazelle, reaches out and hooks it with its large curved **dewclaw**, knocking it off balance. It then grasps its victim with a strangling bite to the neck.

10 After less than a minute of high-speed running, the cheetah is exhausted. It's panting intensely, and its body temperature is heading towards 41 degrees Celsius (105 degrees Fahrenheit). But it continues to suffocate the gazelle.

11 Twenty minutes later the cheetah's breathing and temperature have returned to normal, and the gazelle is dead.

A CHEETAH WORK OUT

Captive cheetahs sometimes suffer from liver problems because their bodies aren't getting enough exercise.

In order to make sure that the cheetahs at one particular zoo still get the all-important intensive one minute work-out they need to stay healthy, the keepers have rigged up a system of pulleys and a steel cable. A dead rabbit is dangled from the pulleys then whizzed across the enclosure. The cheetahs then race after the rabbit at their top speeds.

A cheetah conservation worker

THEY'RE OFF!

During the 1930s cheetahs were raced against greyhounds at the Romford Greyhound Stadium in London. The cheetahs were trained using the same sort of electric hare that was used to train greyhounds and whippets. Needless to say, despite the greyhounds being giving a head start, the cheetahs left them standing.

SAVING WILD CHEETAHS FROM EXTINCTION

Where cheetahs live in the wild in Namibia, the Cheetah Conservation Fund works with local farmers in order to protect farm animals from them. They also work to protect the cheetahs from farmers who, in the past, poisoned or shot them on sight. They do this by encouraging the farmers to let more prey species live on their land so that the cheetahs have plenty of potential victims and are less likely to eat their cattle, sheep and goats. The Cheetah Conservation Fund is also encouraging farmers to use enormous Anatolian shepherd dogs to guard their flocks from cheetahs without actually hurting the big cats.

4 JAGUARS

THE JUNGLE GOD

Two thousand years ago native South American Indians, awestruck by the fabulous jaguar, carved enormous statues of jaguar heads and created giant mosaics of jaguar gods.

Native South American 'witch doctors', known as shamans, perform ceremonies in which they paint their faces with spots and wear jaguar skins and claws, then actually attempt to 'become' jaguars, eating raw meat, sleeping on the ground and avoiding fire, so that they can communicate with the spirit world through the soul of the jaguar.

A native South American witch doctor

JAGUAR COUNTRY

Jaguars live in Central and South American countries including Brazil, Venezuela, Peru, Guatemala, Bolivia and northern Argentina. There were jaguars in Arizona, Texas and New Mexico until the early 20th century, but most of them have disappeared.

There are about 15,000 jaguars in South America and most of them live in dense tropical forests, although some live in marshy grasslands. Most jaguars can be found near swamps and rivers as they like to live close to water which they use for cooling off in hot weather.

A BONE-CRUNCHING, SKULL-SMASHING, APEX PREDATOR!

Like all the big cats, the jaguar is an apex predator. In other words they're at the top of the food chain. By killing all the creatures they do, jaguars keep down populations of animals which may otherwise get out of control.

Rather than chasing prey as cheetahs and lions do, jaguars are what are known as stalk and **ambush** predators. The name jaguar comes from the Native American word *yaguar*, which means *he who kills with one leap*. Jaguars aren't too choosy about what they eat and prey on a whopping eighty plus different sorts of animals including the caiman (which looks a bit like an alligator), sloths, monkeys, turtles, cows, tapirs, deer, frogs, mice, armadillos, dogs, foxes and anacondas (a type of snake).

And because they have the strongest bite of all big cats, twice as strong as that of a lion, their massive jaws can chomp through the armour plating of armadillos, smash huge cow bones and crack open turtle shells! Sometimes, if they can't be bothered to crack open a turtle's shell they simply reach under it and scoop out the living animal's flesh with their huge claws. Yuck!

As well as killing large animals with a deadly neck or throat bite, jaguars are able to bite right through the really thick skulls of horses and cattle, penetrating their brains with their massive teeth. Also, unlike other big cats which start eating the prey's hindquarters first, jaguars begin on the head and shoulders, often leaving the hindquarters uneaten if they're full up.

Jaguars even eat fierce-looking caiman

It's tough but tasty

TALL JAGUAR TAILS

Jaguars also feed on fish, and native South American Indians say that the jaguars tap the surface of the water with their tails to imitate the sound of falling fruit in order to lure fruit-eating fish to them.

They also say that jaguars actually spit into rivers to attract fish then flip them out of the water with their claws. However, most experts believe that these are just folk tales.

NATURE IN THE 'ROAR'

Just like the early versions of the high-performance cars which are named after them, jaguars have a really loud roar which explorers and naturalists describe as sounding just like a rumble of thunder. When they're planning on getting together for some **reproductive** 'hanky-panky' (as top zoologists refer to it), male and female jaguars roar back and forth at each other for as long as two hours.

Beautiful but deadly

SAVING THEIR SKINS... LITERALLY!

The jaguar's lovely spotted fur makes it one of the most beautiful animals in the world but the downside of this is that ruthless people hunt it for its coat. In the past, thousands and thousands of these magnificent creatures have been slaughtered for their skins.

However, jaguars are now totally protected and selling their body parts is against the law. But this still doesn't stop people shooting them, poisoning them and destroying their habitat by logging and **deforestation**. Cattle farmers are also responsible for destroying jaguars. To protect their animals from these big cats, some employ full-time jaguar hunters.

All sorts of schemes are being carried out by conservationists in order to save jaguars from extinction. In Calakmul, Mexico, jaguars are tracked down by conservationists with hunting hounds, which chase them into trees where they're **tranquilised** with darts. They're then weighed, measured and fitted with radio collars. This means the conservationists can find the jaguars at any time and monitor their health and well-being (while the jaguars enjoy non-stop drive-time radio). Some jaguars though, survive without the protection of humans, purely because they live in rainforest so dense and remote that nobody has been able to penetrate it.

Night prowler

An environmental disaster

OBSESSION... FOR JAGUARS

Believe it or not, scientists and conservationists in the South American country of Guatemala use perfume to lure jaguars to hidden cameras so that they can film and study them, in order to be better able to protect them in the wild.

And the jaguars find it irresistible, pawing, sniffing and rubbing themselves against everything which has been sprayed with it! As the jaguars rub their cheeks against objects soaked in the fragrance, they leave their **DNA** and hairs on it which the scientists are then able to use for research. They have also managed to film jaguars mating.

JAGUARS: FAST FACTS

Where they live: South and Central America

Habitat: mainly rainforests and swampy places

Length: 1.1 to 1.8 metres (3.8 to 6 feet)

Tail length: 45 to 75 centimetres (18 to 30 inches)

Weight: males 54 kilograms (120 pounds), females 32 kilograms (70 pounds)

Life span: 12 to 15 years in the wild, up to 20 years in zoos

Number of young at birth: average 2

Size at birth: 700 to 900 grams (1.5 to 2 pounds)

Status: near threatened

South and Central America

5 PUMAS

THE GREAT CAT OF THE AMERICAS

The puma has the largest geographic range of any land animal in the western hemisphere. In other words, they really do get about, and can be found in the snow-covered mountains of Canada, the dense tropical Amazonian rainforest and the semi-desert scrublands of Arizona, to name just a few of their habitats.

Puma here, puma there, pumas, everywhere!

'MEDIUM CAT' HEAD, 'BIG CAT' BODY

Pumas are about the same size as human grown-ups, and including their tails, range from one and a half to two and a half metres (five to eight feet) long, and weigh between 27 to 100 kilograms (60 and 225 pounds). The males are always bigger than the females. They're an odd mixture of medium cat and big cat, with a narrow, short head, like a bobcat or lynx, and a large powerful body like that of a jaguar. They can run very fast, but only over short distances, because of their relatively small lungs. However, their unusually long hind legs enable them to perform massive leaps, as high as six metres (20 feet) up a cliff face, which is the height of some two storey houses, and over 12 metres (40 feet) downhill!

THE CAT OF ONE COLOUR

The puma's Latin name, *Puma Concolor* means *cat of one colour*, and describes the puma's coat which is usually a regular shade ranging from tan to grey to chocolate brown. However, the darker and more reddish coloured pumas tend to come from warmer places such as the tropical rainforests of South America. Like lion cubs, puma kittens are born with spots but as they grow up they lose them (yes, just like teenagers).

When the explorer, Christopher Columbus (1451-1506), arrived in America and first saw a puma, he called it a lion because its coat was the same colour as the African lions he'd already seen. Later explorers felt really puzzled whenever they saw these American 'lions'. They never had manes, so they thought the males must be very, very shy!

A spotty puma kitten

A SCREAM TO MAKE YOUR HAIR STAND ON END!

Unlike lions, tigers, jaguars and leopards, pumas are unable to roar. But female pumas do let out a blood-curdling scream in order to alert local male pumas to the fact that that they're in the mood for '*lurve*'. Imagine what you'd feel like if you were out in the forest one night and you heard this heart-stopping sound:

www.hdw-inc.com/cougarsounds.wav

Puma kittens also make short, sharp 'peep' noises when they're frightened and adult pumas sometimes make low 'whistles' when they're hunting.

WHAT'S IN A NAME?

Pumas hold the Guinness Book of Records world title for being the animal with the highest number of different names.

They are known by at least 40 different ones including cougar, ghost walker, swamp devil, mountain lion, ghost cat, panther, screamer, devil cat, catamount, (which means cat on a mountain), American lion, night crawler, Mexican lion and deer tiger. And that's just in the English language! The reason for this is the fact that they once lived all over the vast continents of North and South America and over the centuries people in different places have come up with their own names for their local big cat. This has also caused a great deal of confusion with many people believing that these are all actually different animals.

PUMAS: FAST FACTS

Where they live: Canada, western USA, Central and South America

Habitat: forests, grasslands and swamps

Length: males 90 centimetres to 1.8 metres (3 to 6 feet), females 90 centimetres to 1.5 metres (3 to 5 feet)

Height at shoulder: 60 to 70 centimetres (1.9 to 2.3 feet)

Weight: males 67 to 103 kilograms (147 to 227 pounds), females 36 to 60 kilograms (79 to 132 pounds)

Life span: up to 20 years

Number of young at birth: usually 3 or 4

Size at birth: 227 to 425 grams (0.5 to 1 pound)

Status: endangered in some places

North America

South America

A 'QUILLING' MACHINE

Pumas eat everything from tiny mice to massive moose, including grasshoppers, raccoons, pigs, bats, frogs, cows, deer and horses, all depending on where they live. Pumas usually eat all of their kill, leaving only the sharp or unpleasant bits such as the hooves and stomach contents. However, they do sometimes swallow whole porcupines and zoologists have found dollops of puma poo made up almost entirely of porcupine quills. Ouch!

Pumas like to attack from above so they'll usually place themselves on a rocky slope or a big boulder before leaping down onto an animal, using both their own weight and the force of gravity to bring it down. But they don't always have it all their own way during attacks and bigger animals, such as elk and deer, will fight back using their hooves and antlers, sometimes even killing the attacking puma.

BURIED ALIVE BY A PUMA!

Pumas sometimes hide their kill by covering it with leaves and sticks to prevent eagles and coyotes from feeding on it, especially if they have cubs. This has led to tales being told by American hunters, trail blazers and similar hairy types, describing how they've gone to sleep on the forest floor only to wake up the next morning and discover that they've been covered with leaves and twigs by a prowling puma, who has mistaken them for dead meat! These days however, most people think these are made-up, 'shaggy cat' stories.

What to eat for dinner? Moose, bat, or porcupine?

PUMAS AND HUMANS

At one time pumas lived all over the South and the North American continents. Many Native American Indians worshipped them and believed they had supernatural powers.

But white settlers in North America had a very different attitude and soon decided that, just like rats and pigeons, pumas were vermin. Hunters were offered up to $40 for each dead puma they brought in, and by the beginning of the 20th century, all of the pumas on the eastern side of North America and Canada had been wiped out.

HUMANS LOOK OUT! PUMA ABOUT!

The ever increasing spread of the human population means that more and more people are moving into puma territory, especially in North America. In order to cut down the chance of people being killed by pumas, local authorities publish puma safety leaflets, which include tips like:

1 Don't ever go hiking alone.

2 Keep your children close. Pumas are more likely to attack children than grown-ups.

3 If you come face to face with a puma, give it a way to escape.

4 Do not run away from a puma. If you have children, pick them up. But do it without bending or turning away from the puma.

5 Try to appear bigger than you are by raising your arms and opening your jacket.

6 Throw sticks and stones at the puma while speaking to it in a loud voice. You must convince it you are not prey and may well be a danger to it.

NEXT 2 MILES

Look, no hands!

6 LEOPARDS

NOW YOU SEE IT...
NOW YOU DON'T

"When the tiger stalks the jungle like the lowering clouds of a thunderstorm, the leopard moves as silently as mist drifting on a dawn wind."

Old Indian proverb

Some people say that the leopard is the ultimate predator. They combine the strength and power of big cats with the incredible agility of smaller ones. They are excellent climbers, superb stalkers, fast runners, cunning and courageous hunters and, most remarkable of all, are totally brilliant at disappearing in the blink of an eye. A leopard can be right next to you and you won't even know it's there!

SUPREME SURVIVORS

Big cat researchers think of leopards as supreme survival artists. They live in almost every sort of habitat, ranging from the sub-freezing mountains of Russia and China to the sweltering, dense tropical jungles of India, and from the savanna grasslands of Africa to the huge Kalahari desert, where they can go without water for more than a week.

Asia

Africa

LEOPARDS: FAST FACTS

Where they live: Asia and Africa

Habitat: forest, grasslands, mountains and deserts

Length: 91 to 191 centimetres (3 to 6 feet)

Tail length: 58 to 110 centimetres (23 to 44 inches)

Weight: males 36 to 90 kilograms (80 to 200 pounds), females 28 to 60 kilograms (62 to 132 pounds)

Life span: 12 to 15 years in the wild, up to 23 years in zoos

Number of young at birth: 2 to 3 on average

Size at birth: 500 grams (1 pound)

Status: near threatened

SMART, STEALTHY, SWIFT, SECRETIVE...

If a leopard took part in the Olympics it would get a gold medal every time!

And if it was recruited by the Secret Service it would make James Bond look like a bumbling amateur!

Leopards are superbly athletic. One was seen to jump over a **ravine** measuring over six and a half metres (22 feet) across. And another was witnessed climbing an enormous tree with a sheer trunk 20 metres (65 feet) in diameter! They also come down these massive tree trunks head first, the mark of a master climber!

The leopard's stealth and secretiveness is unbelievable. In 1990 three leopards were found living in an abandoned steam engine in the busy railway station right in the centre of the city of Kampala in the African country of Uganda. And when a leopard escaped from its enclosure in Nairobi in Kenya, the rangers who were brought in to track it, not only found its footprints in parks and gardens, but the footprints of two other leopards which had obviously been living in the city centre, completely undetected by thousands of people going about their daily business.

And the Olympic gold goes to... the leopard!

A black leopard

IS IT A LEOPARD, OR A 'PANTHER'?

Leopards have long bodies, large skulls and, compared to the other big cats, relatively short legs. They look a little bit like jaguars but are slightly smaller and the flower-shaped **rosettes** on their fur are smaller and closer together than a jaguar's. As with jaguars, some leopards appear to be completely black. But look at them closely (if you dare), and you'll see that their rosette markings are still visible.

PUTTING ON A BIT OF WEIGHT

Leopards hunt mainly at night and will sometimes walk as far as 20 kilometres (12 miles) in search of prey. When they've pinpointed a victim they'll get down on their bellies and wriggle towards it silently, freezing if they think it has sensed their presence.

Then, when they're close enough, they pounce, killing their victim with a bite to its throat. Very occasionally, they'll leap onto their prey from a tree. One male leopard was seen to leap from a tree onto the back of an eland bull which was ten times its own weight!

In order to hide their meals from hyenas and other **scavengers**, once a leopard's made its kill, it will often climb into a tree with its victim, even though the kill weighs three times more than it does. It will then tuck in, eating huge amounts of meat in one go. After a leopard's eaten its kill it's sometimes an enormous 20 per cent heavier than it was when it started. Imagine that! You normally weigh five stone, but after you've finished your dinner... you're six stone!

When they're hunting monkeys, leopards will cunningly pretend to climb the tree the monkeys are in. This makes the monkeys panic and brings them scampering to the ground which means they're easy meat for the leopard, saving it the trouble of actually climbing the tree!

Here, little monkeys!

LEOPARD SKIN LOOKS BEST ON LEOPARDS

In some places leopards are an endangered species and in others they're considered to be a pest. The stunningly beautiful skin of a leopard was once regarded as a fashion must-have item and a status symbol. Sadly, in some places, it still is.

In the past, glamorous film stars proudly strutted around in coats made from leopard skin, giving no thought to the fact that a magnificent animal had been cruelly slaughtered just so that they could look cool.

In fact, in the early 1960s, poachers are estimated to have killed 50,000 leopards in East Africa, just to keep up with the demand for these high fashion items. The sale of leopard skin was banned in 1975 and these days most people prefer to see leopard skin coats being worn by leopards. But poaching still goes on, not only for leopard skin, but for leopards' teeth, claws, bones and whiskers which are used as ingredients in Asian medicines.

Some **herdsman** also hunt leopards to protect their animals from them. However, on the positive side, some farmers are finally realising that leopards do a good job by eating animals like baboons and wild pigs which destroy their crops.

The deadly price of fashion

7 SNOW LEOPARDS

THE SHAPE CHANGER

Very few people have ever seen a snow leopard in the wild. So stealthy are they that mountain people in Central Asia describe them as shape-changing spirits. These secretive creatures live in the highest, coldest and most inhospitable environments in the world, where the air is so lacking in oxygen that many humans could only survive for a few hours.

But snow leopards are perfectly **adapted** to survive in these extreme conditions. Their short broad noses with their very large nasal cavities immediately warm up the freezing mountain air before it gets to their lungs. Their thick, **insulating** coats keep them warm. Their huge paws act like snowshoes so they can walk through snow up to a metre deep, and their enormous tails, as heavy as anchor rope and often up to a metre (three feet) long, act as balances as they leap huge distances. When it gets really cold they wrap their hugely thick and soft tails around themselves for warmth, just as we would do with a scarf.

If a human did manage to get close to a snow leopard they probably wouldn't even know it was there. The coat of this super-stealthy cat with its silver-white fur and smoky grey and blurred black markings provides perfect camouflage against snow-covered slopes and mountain cliff-faces, enabling them to vanish like a swirl of mist.

Snow leopards in their element

MOUNTAIN HUNTER

Snow leopards normally hunt sheep, mountain goats, game birds, small rodents and marmots. However, in the coldest weather, when many prey animals are hibernating, **they will often go further down the mountain to prey on domestic livestock, which brings them into conflict with herders and farmers.**

However, there are very few records of snow leopards attacking humans and people who care for them say that they soon become tame and gentle in captivity. In fact, small shepherd boys are able to drive snow leopards from their kill just by waving a stick at them (please don't try this at home).

THE VANISHING CAT

Snow leopards have always been rare but now they're getting rarer. Their habitats are being destroyed, they're being killed by farmers and their prey animals are being hunted by humans. However, organisations like the Snow Leopard Trust are trying to stop them from becoming extinct by supporting the herders whose flocks snow leopards occasionally prey on.

Ready to pounce

SNOW LEOPARDS: FAST FACTS

Where they live: the mountains of Central Asia

Habitat: cliffs, rocky slopes and forests

Body length: 99 to 130 centimetres (39 to 51 inches), females slightly smaller

Tail length: 79 centimetres to 1 metre (31 to 40 inches)

Shoulder height: 60 centimetres (24 inches)

Weight: males 45 to 55 kilograms (99 to 121 pounds), females 35 to 40 kilograms (77 to 88 pounds)

Lifespan: unknown in the wild but in zoos up to 18 years

Number of young at birth: average 2

Weight at birth: 320 to 708 grams (0.7 to 1.5 pounds)

Status: endangered

Asia

8 CLOUDED LEOPARDS

THE LEOPARD THAT'S NOT A LEOPARD

Clouded leopards are probably even rarer and more shy than snow leopards, which is why most people have never seen one, either in the wild or a zoo. And they weren't even recorded as a species until 1821!

Clouded leopards live in the wild in Southeast Asia and get their name from the cloud-shaped spots on their fur. In China they're known as *mint leopards* because their markings are shaped like mint leaves and in Malaysia they're called *tree tigers*. And, surprisingly, some zoologists believe that they aren't actually a leopard, but a separate species of cat in their own right.

In size, they're somewhere between a small cat and a big cat. They purr like the small cats, but also moan, roar, chuff, growl, hiss and meow. And, just to make them even more unique, the pupils of their eyes never get fully round like a big cats' do, and also never shrink to vertical slits like small cats' do, they just remain oblong.

They also have the longest tail of any cat in relation to the size of their body! And then there are their teeth which at two inches long, are as big as a tiger's! These massive gnashers often lead to clouded leopards being described as a modern-day descendant of the **sabre-tooth tiger**. And just to make room for those super-choppers, in relation to the size of its body, a clouded leopard can open its jaws wider than any other big cat.

Time for a tasty snack

THE FANTASTIC CLIMBING CAT

Clouded leopards are brilliant climbers. They can climb down a vertical tree trunk headfirst, make their way along branches by hanging beneath them like a sloth, and even hang from branches by just their hind feet.

And all this means they can move through treetops grabbing hold of the birds, squirrels and monkeys which form part of their diet. Clouded leopards also kill deer, and wild pigs by dropping down on them from treetops, which must come as a very nasty surprise to the deer and pigs.

The cat that thinks it's a monkey

CLOUDED LEOPARDS: FAST FACTS

Southeast Asia

Where they live: Southeast Asia

Habitat: mostly tropical rainforest, sometimes grasslands and wetlands

Length: 1.4 metres (3 feet) long

Tail length: 1.4 metres (3 feet)

Height at shoulders: 25 to 40 centimetres (10 to 16 inches)

Weight: males 20 to 27 kilograms (45 to 60 pounds), females 11 to 14 kilograms (25 to 30 pounds)

Life span: average 11 years, up to 19 years in zoos

Number of young at birth: average 2

Weight at birth: 170 grams (0.4 pounds)

Status: vulnerable

NOT SO BIG CATS

CARACALS

Caracals are the jump-jets of the wild cat world! They can leap an amazing three metres (ten feet) into the air from a vertical take-off and can even change direction mid-jump! Using this technique they're able knock fast flying birds to the ground.

Caracals are such brilliant bird hunters that they've been used at airports in order to scare away birds which might otherwise fly into aircraft engines and cause crashes.

Caracals' black, funnel-shaped ears are controlled by about twenty muscles which enable them to operate like furry feline satellite dishes, listening out for the slightest sound which might indicate that there is prey nearby. The movements of a caracal's ears can also tell you a lot about what it's up to:

Stiff and pointing straight up = listening out for prey

Relaxed pointing forwards and outwards = resting

Flat, straight back against head = frightened

Turned back but not completely flat = about to attack

Not impressed? Well, you try moving your ears into all those different positions!

Go on, I'm all ears!

CARACALS: FAST FACTS

Africa

Where they live: Africa and the Middle East to India

Habitat: savanna, semi-desert, woodlands, steppe and mountains

Body length: 59 to 106 centimetres (23 to 42 inches)

Shoulder height: 46 centimetres (18 inches)

Weight: males 11.5 to 18 kilograms (25 to 40 pounds), females 9.5 to 11 kilograms (21 to 24 pounds)

Life span: up to 12 years in the wild, up to 17 years in zoos

Number of young at birth: average 3

Weight at birth: 400 grams (0.8 pounds)

Status: lower risk than other wild cats. Nevertheless the population is declining due to habitat loss and hunting by humans

THE LYNX AND THE BOBCAT

The lynx is a medium-size wildcat with a short tail and tufts of black hair on the tips of its ears. It can be found in European and Siberian forests, Canadian forests and tundra regions. There are also lynx in southern Spain but sadly they're now almost extinct in the region.

About 100 years ago, there were over 10,000 lynx in Spain and Portugal, but now less than 200 remain. However, many people are keen to see their numbers increase again, including a Spanish woman who recently left a whopping two and a half million pounds in her will to help protect the *Iberian* lynx, as it's known.

Lynx also used to live in Britain but were hunted to extinction 500 years ago. However, there is now a plan to reintroduce them as a way of culling many of the two million deer which eat valuable farm crops.

I'm the lynx that slinks

The bobcat is a sort of lynx which is about the same size as a cocker spaniel but much more muscular with longer legs (and would definitely eat the cocker spaniel for breakfast). They're called bobcats because their tail looks as if it has been cut off or 'bobbed'. They live in forests, swamps, deserts and mountainous areas in Canada, the USA and Mexico.

Just bobbing along!

THE BOBCAT BLUES

Bobcats are crepuscular and, like all cats, they mark their territory by scratching tree trunks, doing lots of very smelly poos and wees (and putting up lots of 'Keep Out – Bobcat About!' notices). They eat small to medium sized animals including rabbits, rats, squirrels, fish, young deer, foxes, sheep and pet cats and dogs. Sadly, they are hunted for their beautiful fur and also for so called 'sport'!

LYNX AND BOBCAT: FAST FACTS

Where they live: North America, Europe, Northern Asia

Habitat: prairies, steppes, forests, tundra

Body length: Siberian lynx up to 1 metre (39 inches); other lynx 48 to 90 centimetres (19 to 35 inches)

Tail length: 10 to 15 centimetres (4 to 6 inches)

Shoulder height: Siberian lynx up to 70 centimetres (27 inches); other lynx 40 to 56 centimetres (16 to 22 inches)

Weight: Siberian lynx males up to 38 kilograms (84 pounds); other lynx 8 to 27 kilograms (18 to 60 pounds)

Life span: About 12 years in the wild; up to 21 years in zoos

Number of young at birth: 2 to 4 kittens

Weight at birth: 128 to 430 grams (4.5 to 15 ounces)

Status: the Iberian lynx is critically endangered

Northern Europe

North America

The lynx effect

OCELOTS HAVE GOT THE LOT

Many wildcat experts say the ocelot is one of the most difficult cats to describe because its stunningly beautiful coat is such a tangle of different patterns. Ocelots are also known as the 'dwarf leopard' because they do look a bit like miniature leopards.

Cat experts also find it really hard to study ocelots because they are so secretive (and often won't even tell you their age or favourite colour). They mainly live in South and Central America and spend their days fast asleep in dense undergrowth. At night they wonder tropical forests, mangrove swamps and savanna grasslands in search of their favourite foods which include rats, mice, frogs, lizards, snakes and iguanas.

Some people, including the surrealist artist, Salvador Dali, have been known to keep ocelots as pets. However, it's not a good idea to keep any wild cat in your home as they generally do not make good pets (especially the man-eaters).

Stripes, smudges, spots and dots!

OCELOT: FAST FACTS

Where they live: Central and South America and Texas

Habitat: rainforest and dry scrubland

Body length: 66 to 100 centimetres (26 to 39 inches)

Tail length: 30 to 45 centimetres (12 to 18 inches)

Weight: 11 to16 kilograms (24 to 35 pounds)

Life span: up to 21 years in zoos, unknown in wild

Number of young at birth: 1 to 4 kittens

Weight at birth: 300 grams (0.6 pounds)

Status: least concern

South America

SERVALS – THEY COULD HEAR A PIN DROP!

Servals, with their large ears, spotted coats and long necks, are sometimes known as the 'giraffe' cat. They have incredibly good hearing and their large ears can even pick up the sounds of small animals busily scurrying around in their underground dens (making cups of tea, doing a bit of dusting, that sort of thing).

Just like caracals, servals perform those incredible three and a half metre 'jump-jet' take-offs which enable them to snatch birds and insects from the air. Servals also 'fish' for animals down their hidey-holes using their incredibly long feet. One serval was seen standing on its back legs poking its front paw into the nest holes of a colony of swallows as it systematically searched for their chicks and eggs.

Some servals have actually learned to use car headlights to help them hunt. When a car passes they stare at the lit-up part of the road then, spotting prey, they bound towards it and pounce! They then, quite sensibly, quickly return to the roadside with their catch.

You can run, but you can't hide

Africa

SERVALS: FAST FACTS

Where they live: Africa, south of the Sahara desert

Habitat: savannas and forests near water

Body length: 70 to 100 centimetres (2.3 to 3.3 feet)

Shoulder height: 45 to 60 centimetres (1.5 to 2 feet)

Weight: 9 to 18 kilograms (19 to 40 pounds)

Life span: up to 19 years

Number of young at birth: 1 to 5

Weight at birth: 250 grams (0.5 pounds)

Status: least concern

ABOUT ZSL

The Zoological Society of London (ZSL) is a charity that provides conservation support for animals both in the UK and worldwide. We also run ZSL London Zoo and ZSL Whipsnade Zoo.

By buying this book, you have helped us to raise money to continue our conservation work with animals around the world.

Find out more at **zsl.org**

FURTHER INFORMATION:

ZSL London Zoo
Outer Circle, Regent's Park,
London, NW1 4RY, UK
www.zsl.org/london

ZSL Whipsnade Zoo
Dunstable, Bedfordshire,
LU6 2LF, UK
www.zsl.org/whipsnade

The Cheetah Conservation Fund
www.cheetah.org

The Snow Leopard Trust
www.snowleopard.org

Lion Guardians
www.lionguardians.wildlifedirect.org

www.storiesfromthezoo.com

GLOSSARY

adapted – when an animal changes to suit its habitat

agile – quick and flexible

ambush – a surprise attack from a hiding place

body language – communication through body movements

coalition – a group or pair working together

conservationist – person who works to protect wildlife and the environment

conservation status – a measure of how close a species is to becoming extinct

cormorant – a sea bird with dark feathers

crepuscular – active in the hours of dawn and dusk

DNA – the genetic instructions that make up all living organisms

dewclaw – a claw on the foot of an animal used only for hunting

deforestation – clearing an area of trees

domain – area that is dominated by one animal or group

exterminate – to destroy completely

extinct – when a species has completely died out

game reserve – area of land where wild animals are protected

geographic range – the area in which a species lives

glucose – a sugar found in food that the body burns to make energy

herdsman – a person whose job is to look after farm animals

hibernating – when animals spend the winter asleep

infrasound – a sound that humans can't hear because the sound waves are going too slowly

inhospitable – difficult and uncomfortable

insulating – to keep out the cold

livestock – farm animals raised for meat and for market such as cattle, sheep and goats

mangrove swamps – boggy areas where mangrove trees grow

menagerie – a collection of unusual or exotic animals

micro-chip – an electronic chip put into the neck of an animal

naturalist – a person who studies nature

nocturnal – awake during the night instead of the day

persecuted – to be harassed and treated badly

predators – animals that hunt and eat other animals

preserving – to protect from harm

prey – an animal hunted for food

prides – a family group of lions

ravine – a narrow valley or gorge

reproductive – to grow in number by mating

retina – a light sensitive part at the back of the eye

retractable – able to withdraw/shrink back

rosettes – rose-like patterns

sabre-tooth tiger – an extinct species of a big cat famous for its huge teeth

scavenger – something that eats animals that are already dead

sinuses – the space inside the head behind the nose

stalk – to follow prey without being seen

territories – areas occupied by a single animal or group

tranquilised – to be given a drug that makes an animal sleepy

vaccinated – to be protected from a disease

zoologists – experts who study animals

INDEX